Red Alert

Hot Sexy Red Lingerie Girls Models Pictures

By **PHOTO ART LOVER**

Copyright © Red Alert

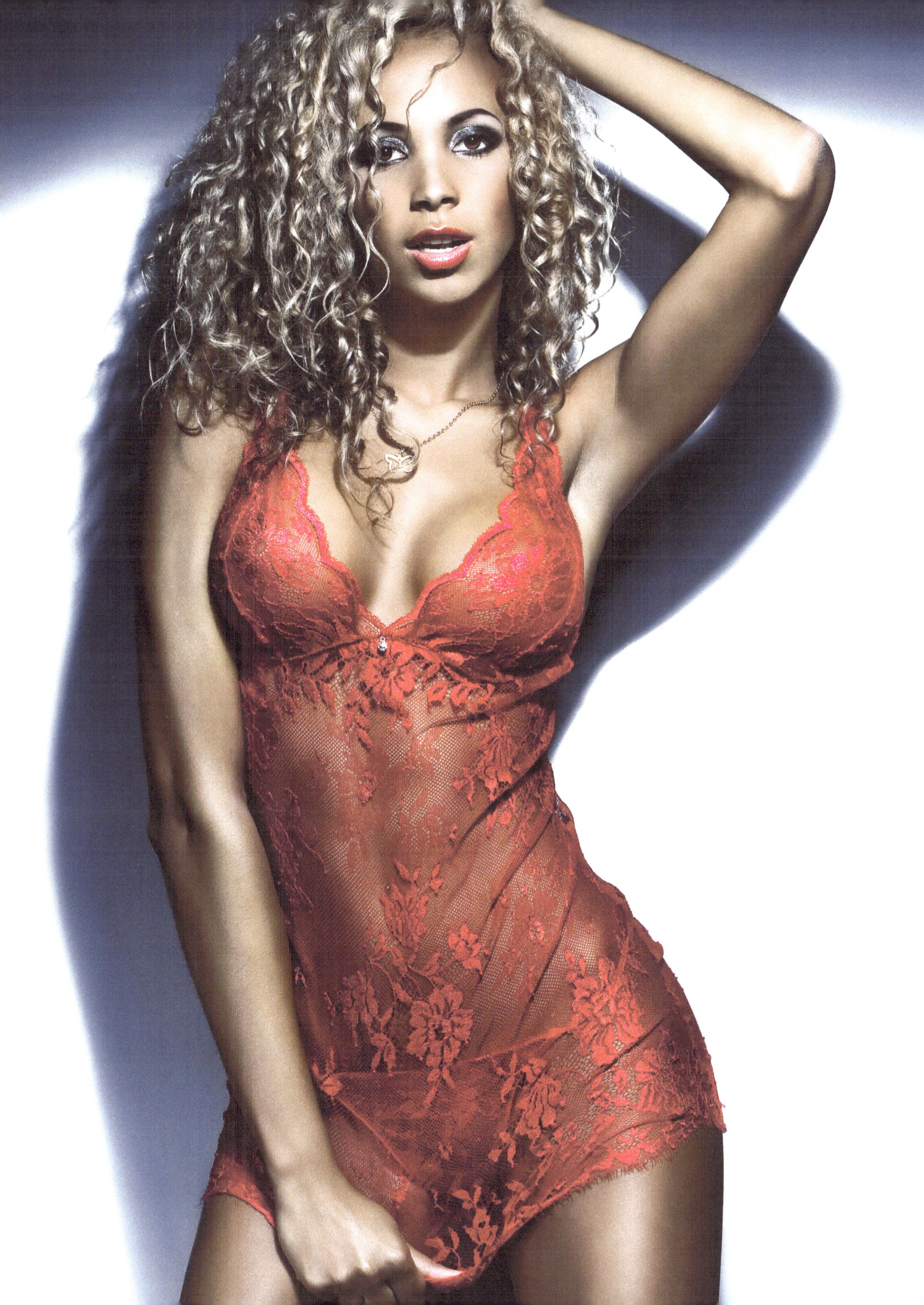

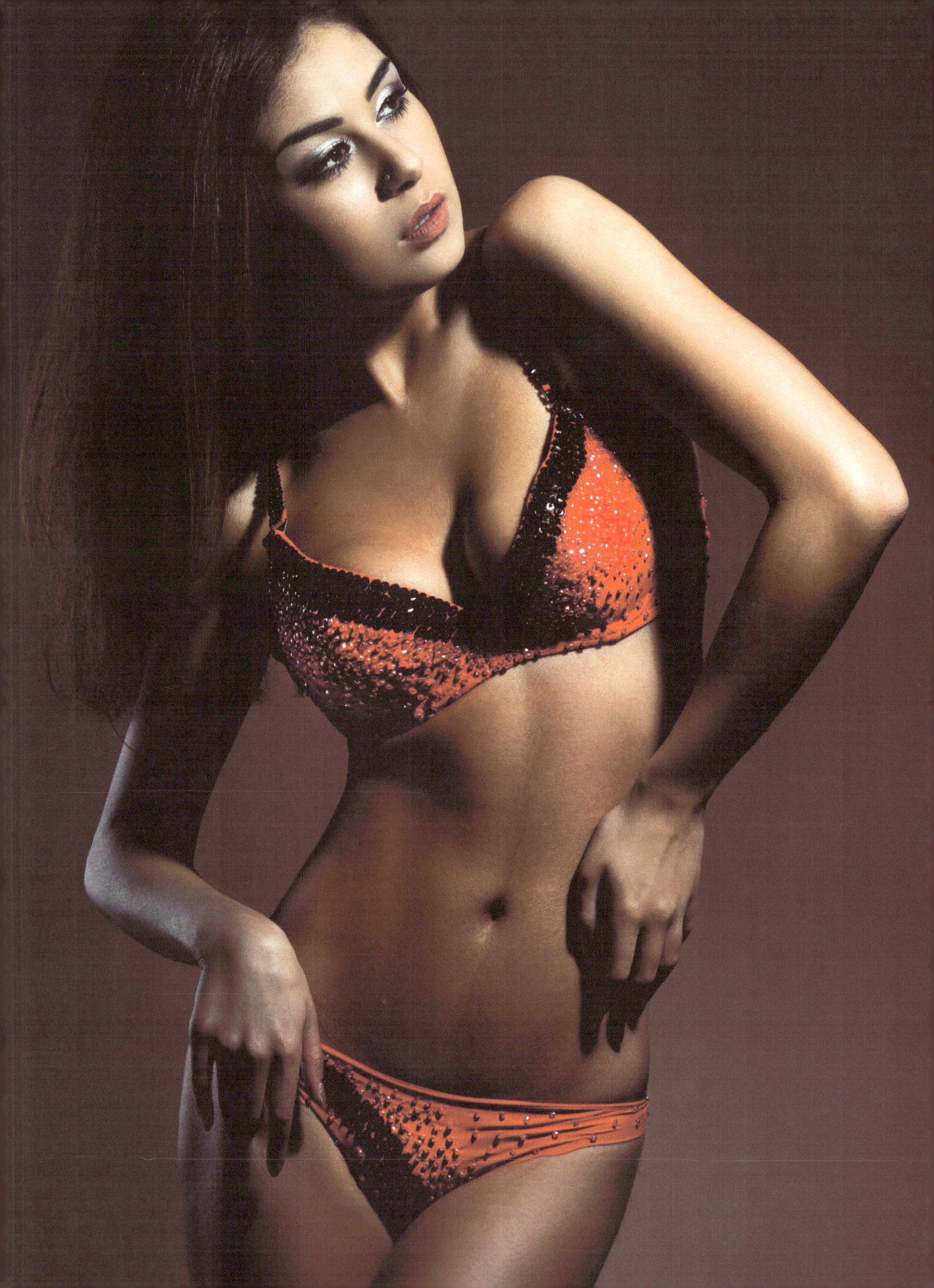

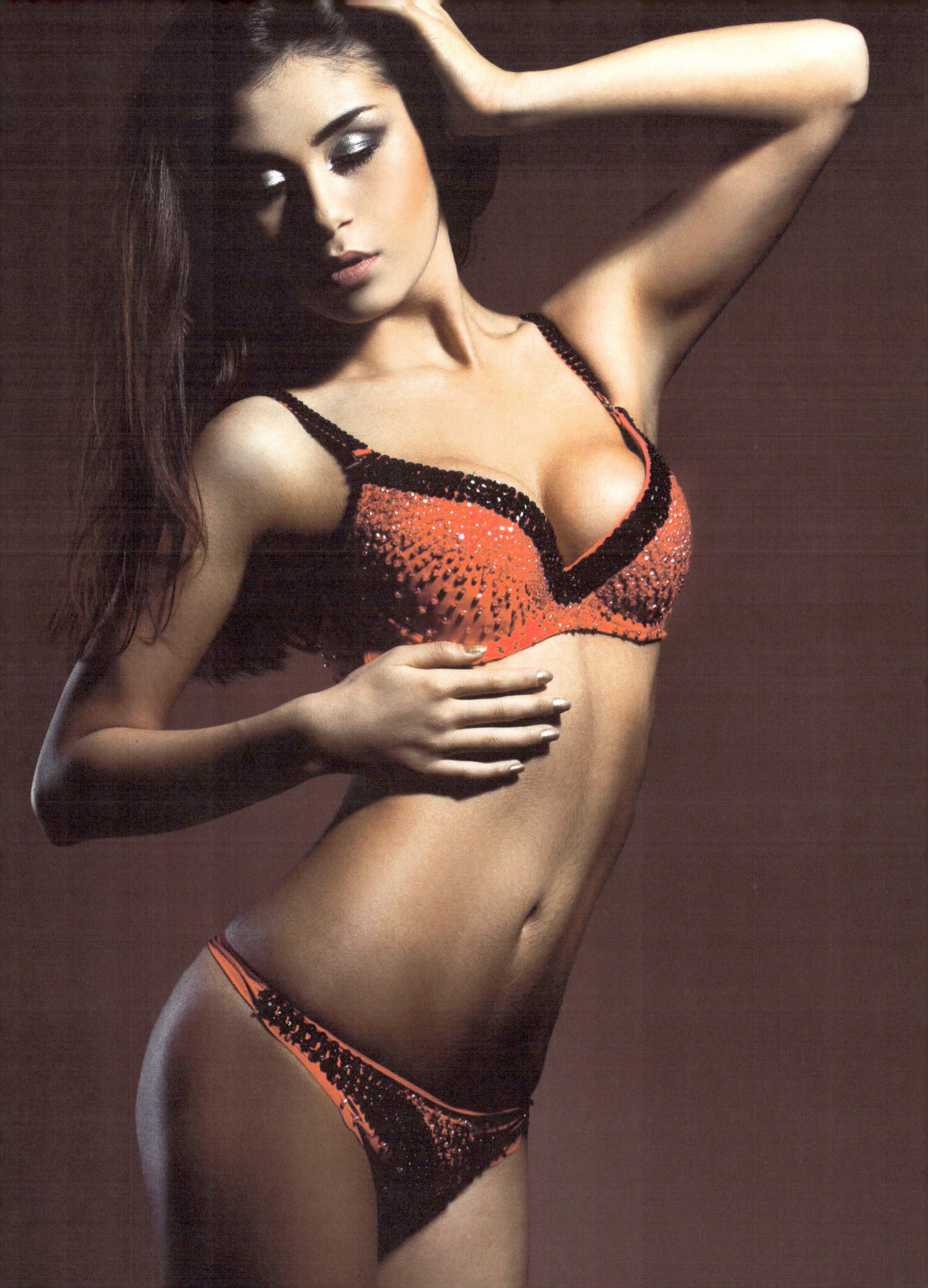

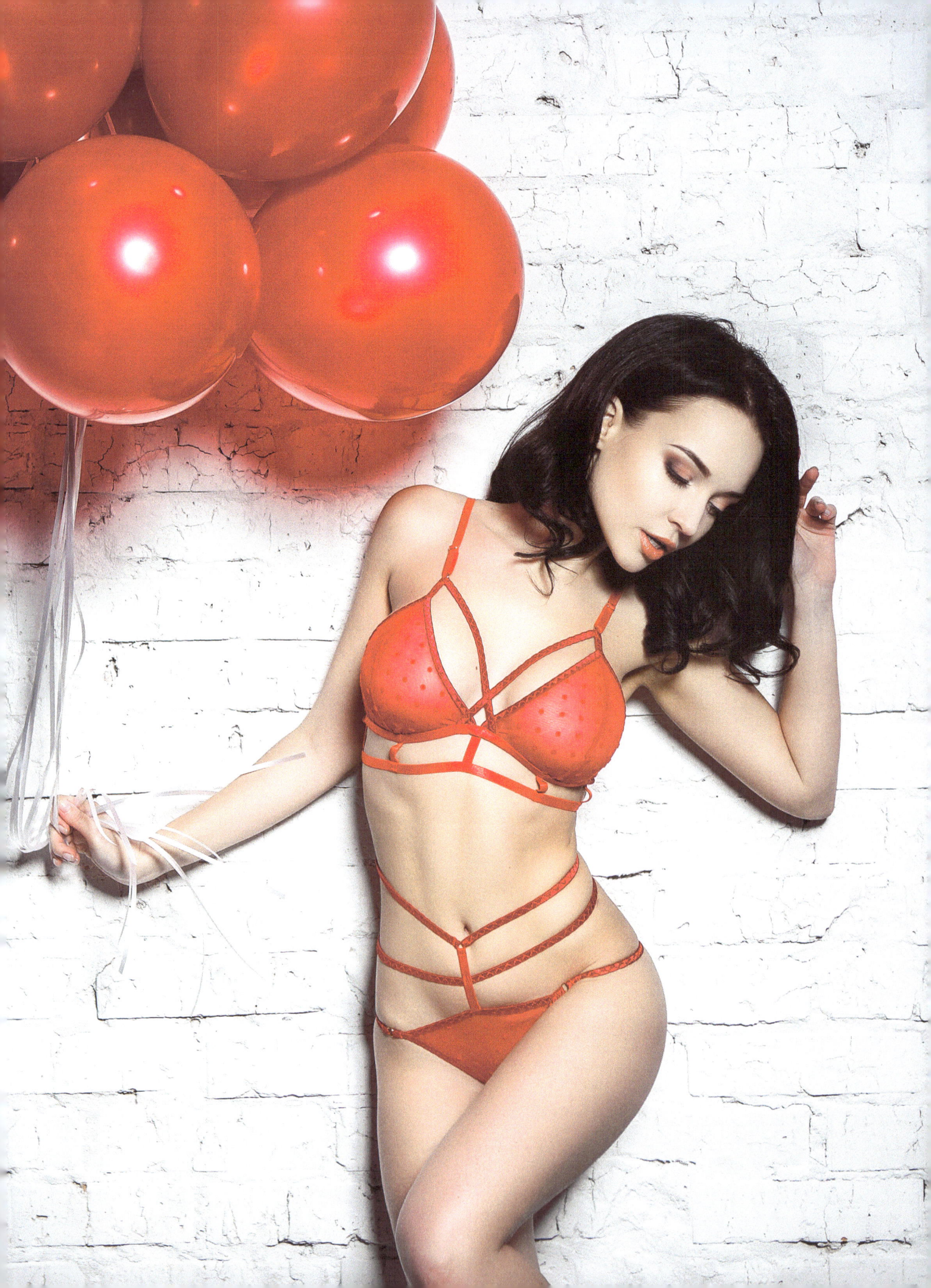

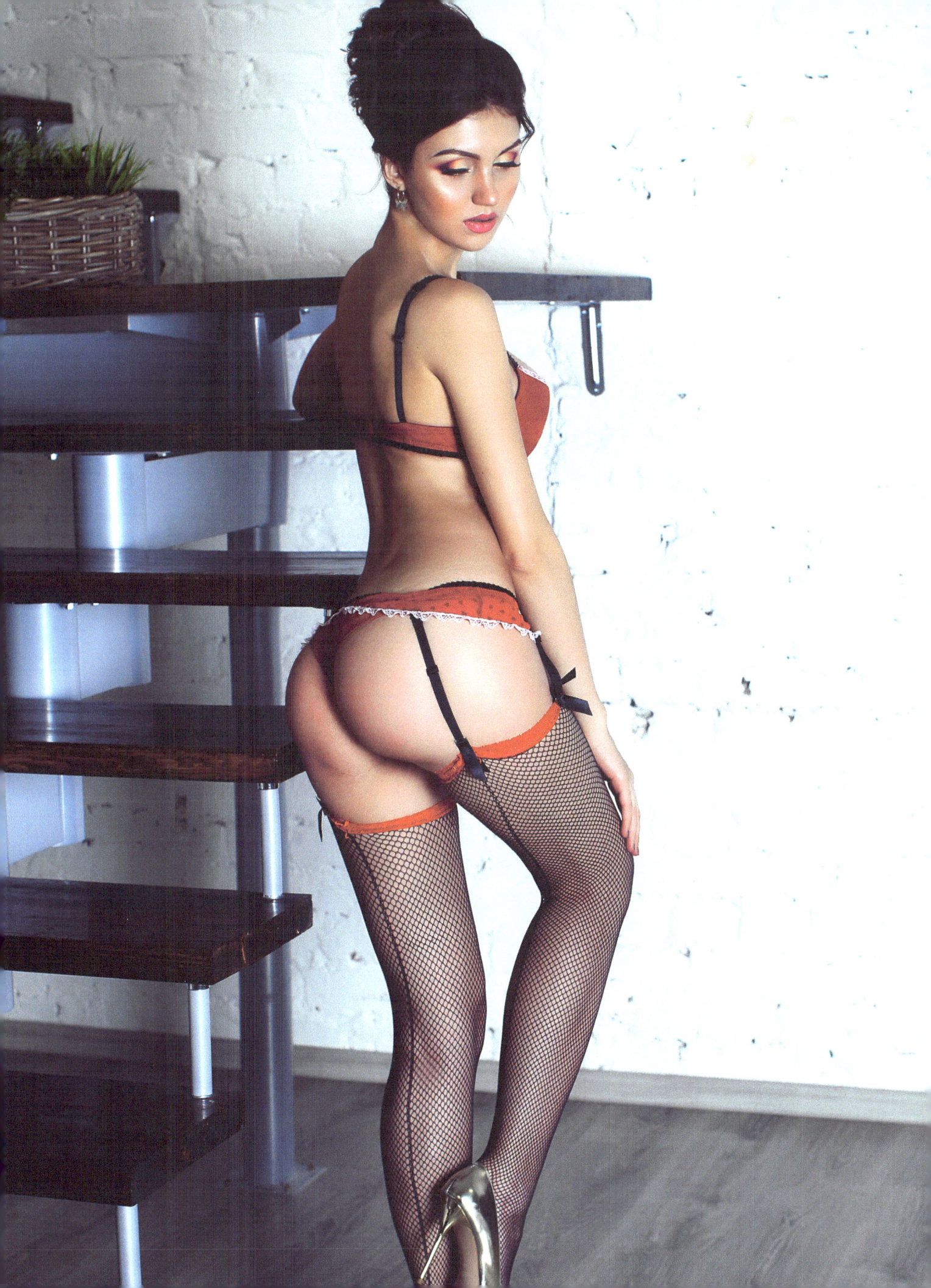

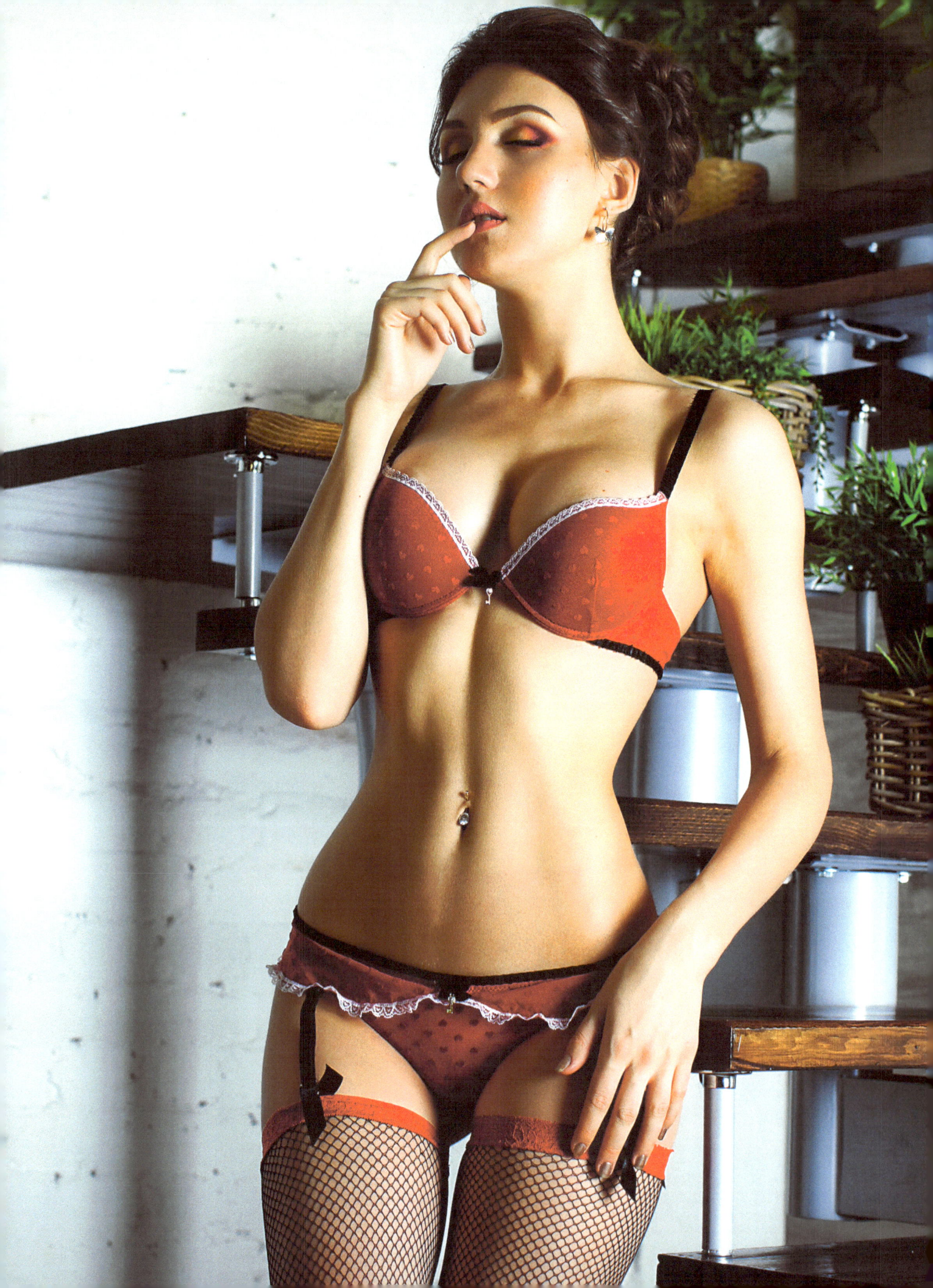

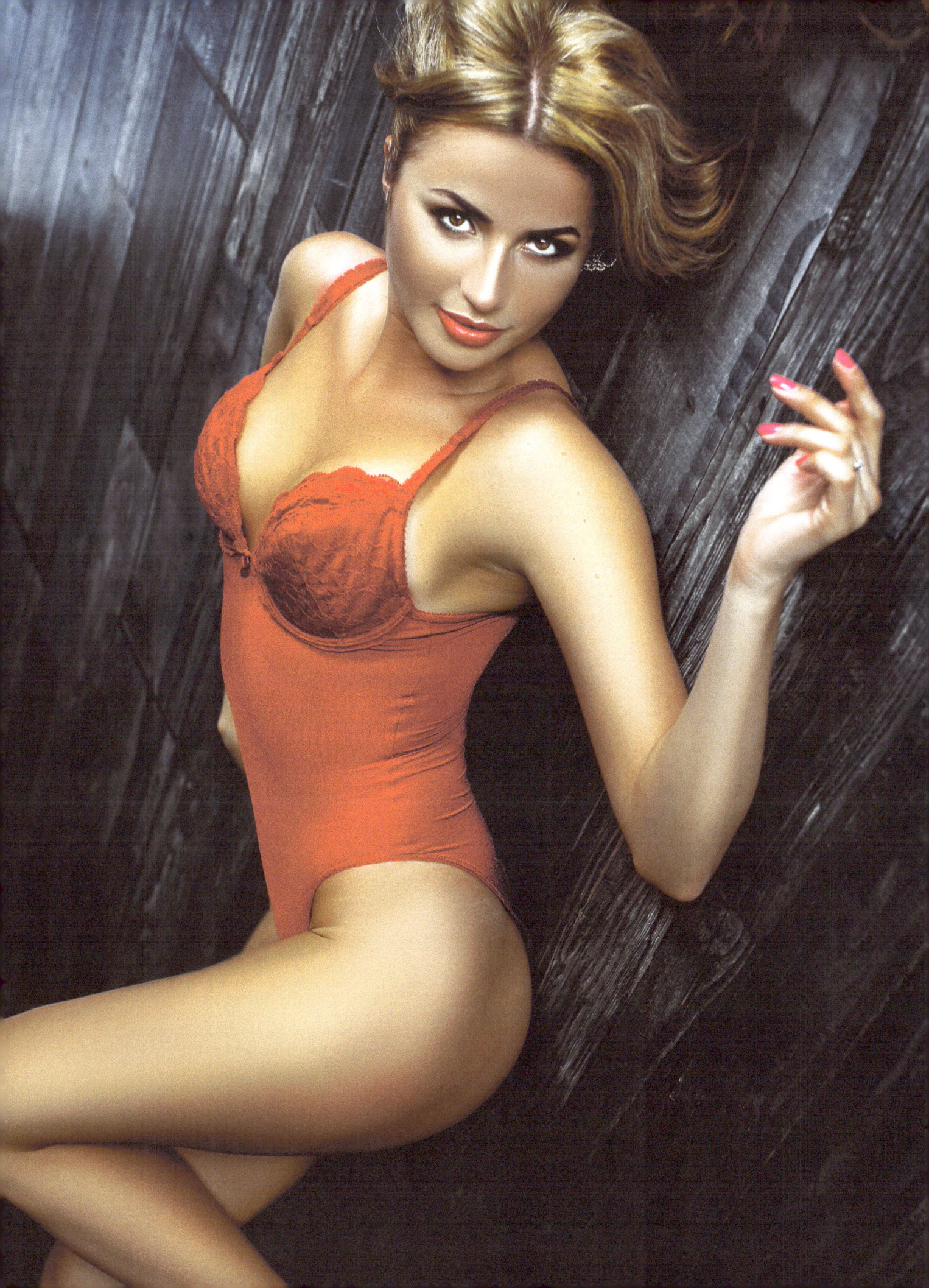

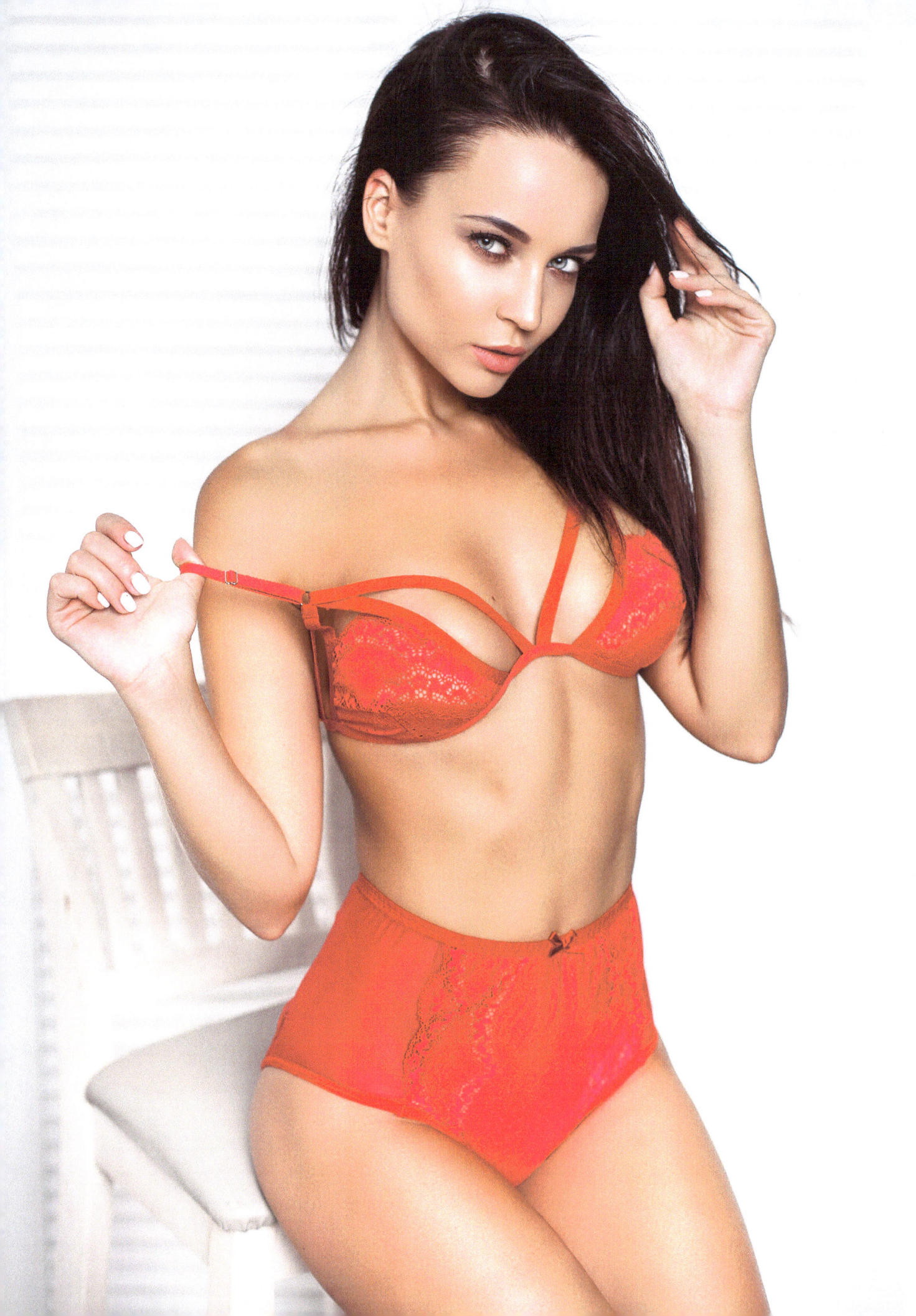

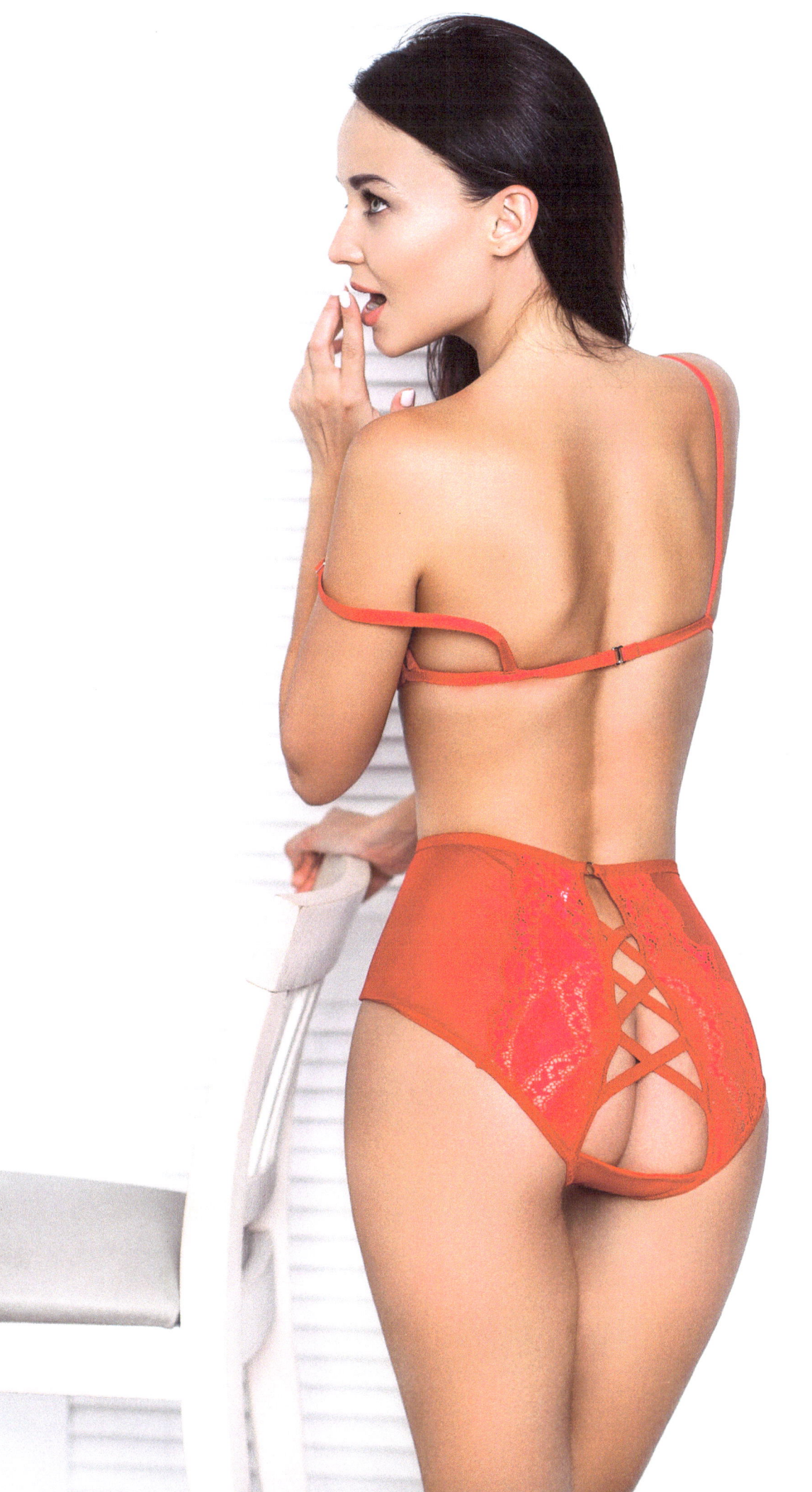

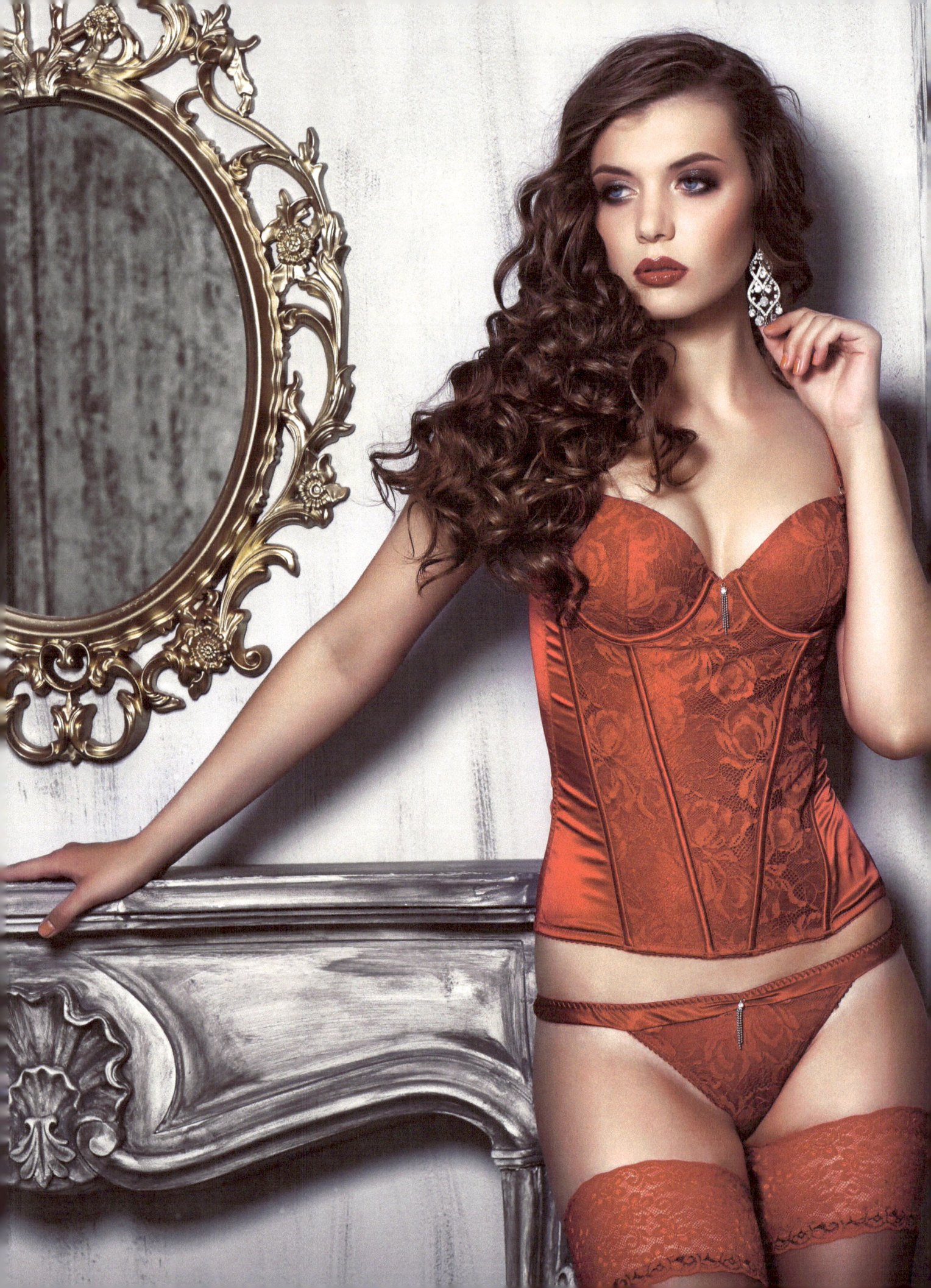

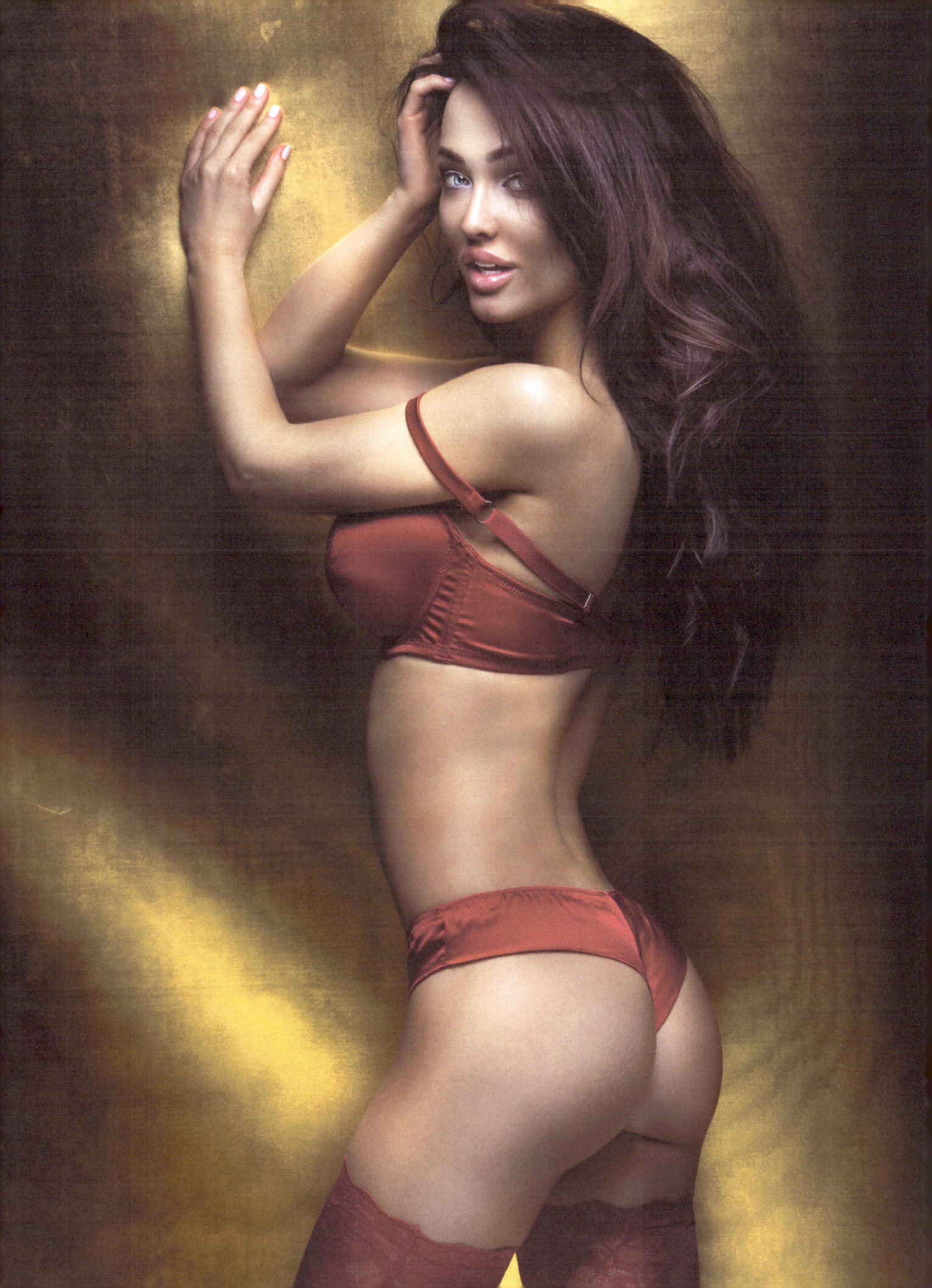

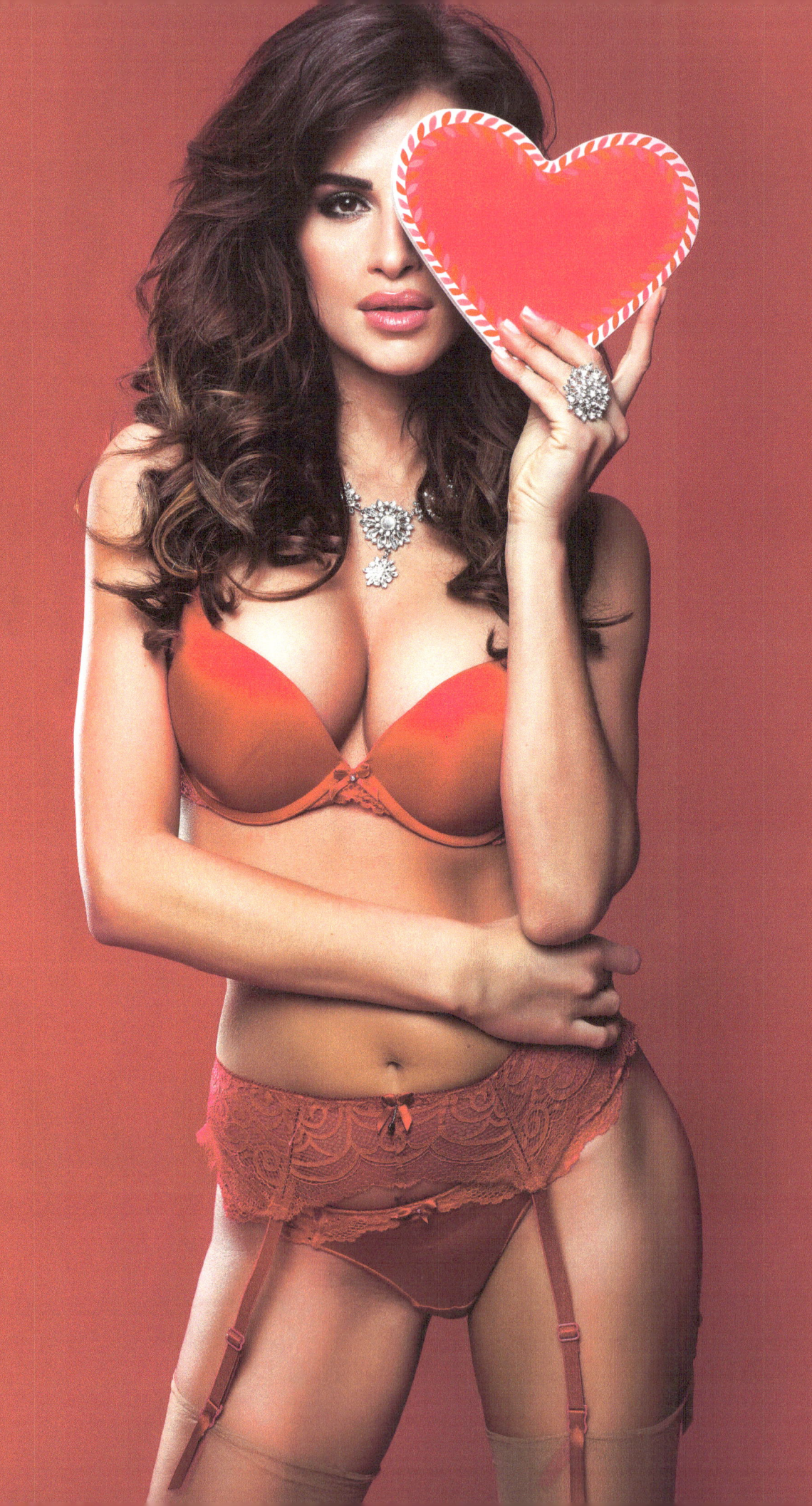

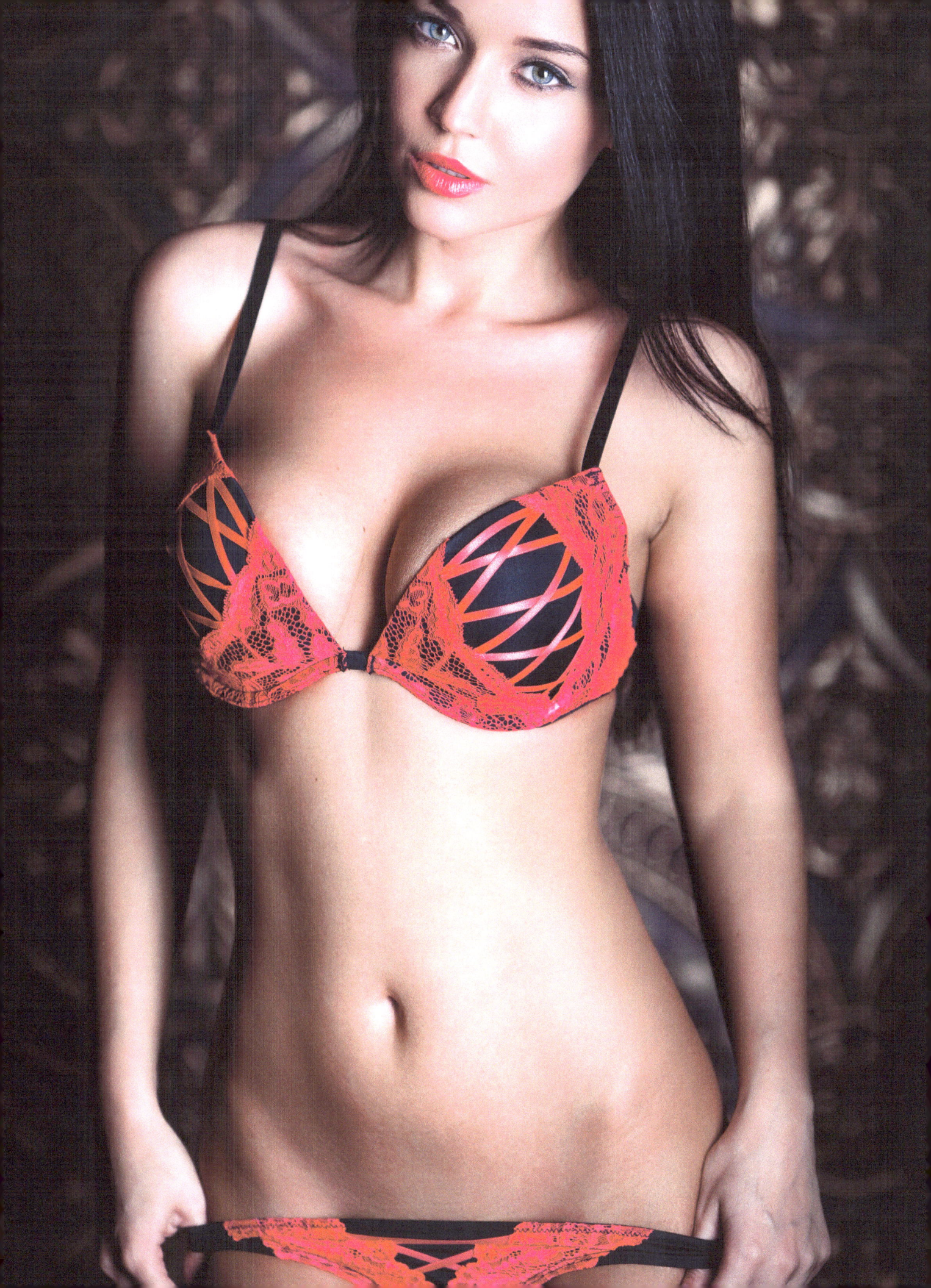

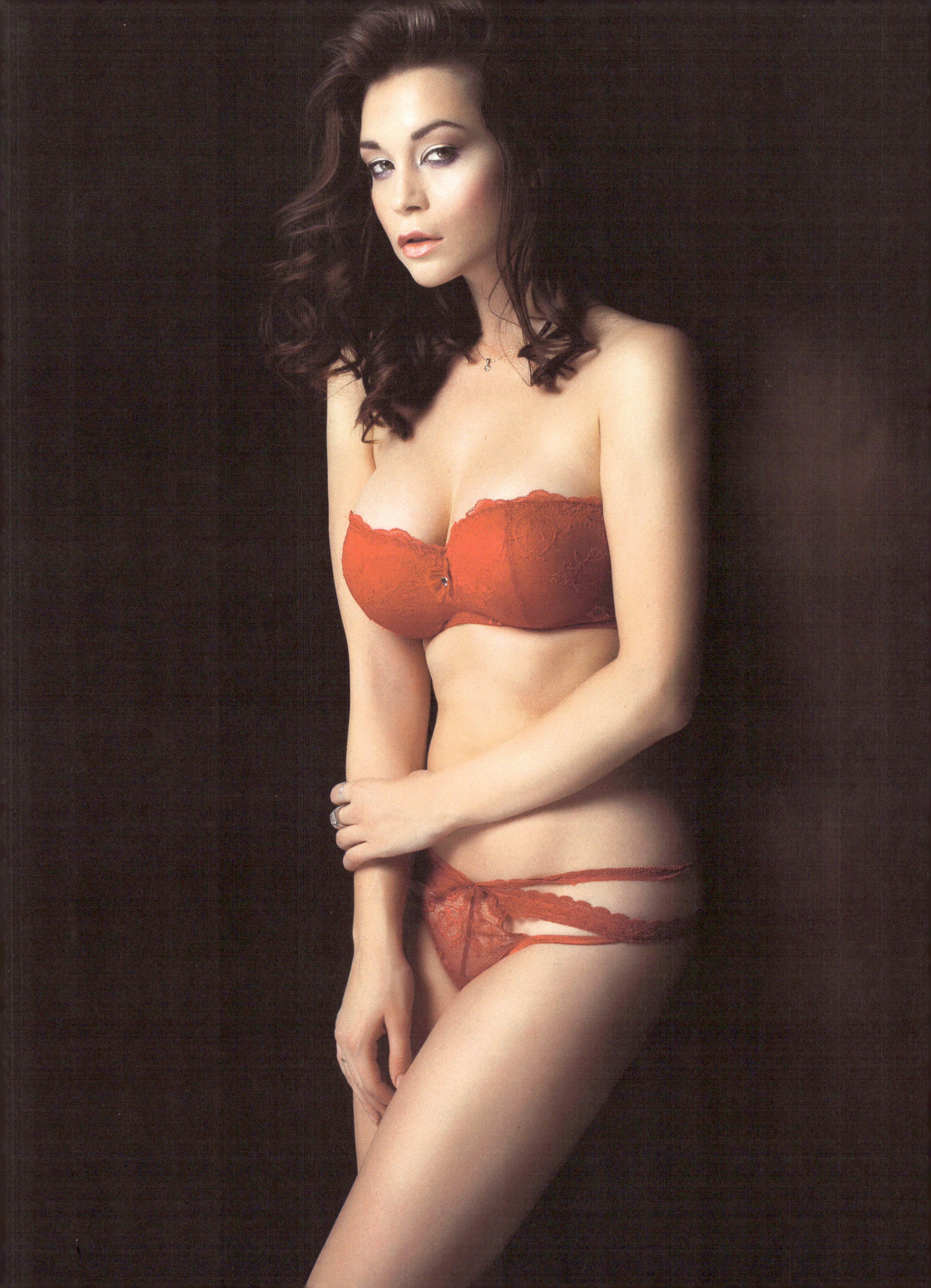

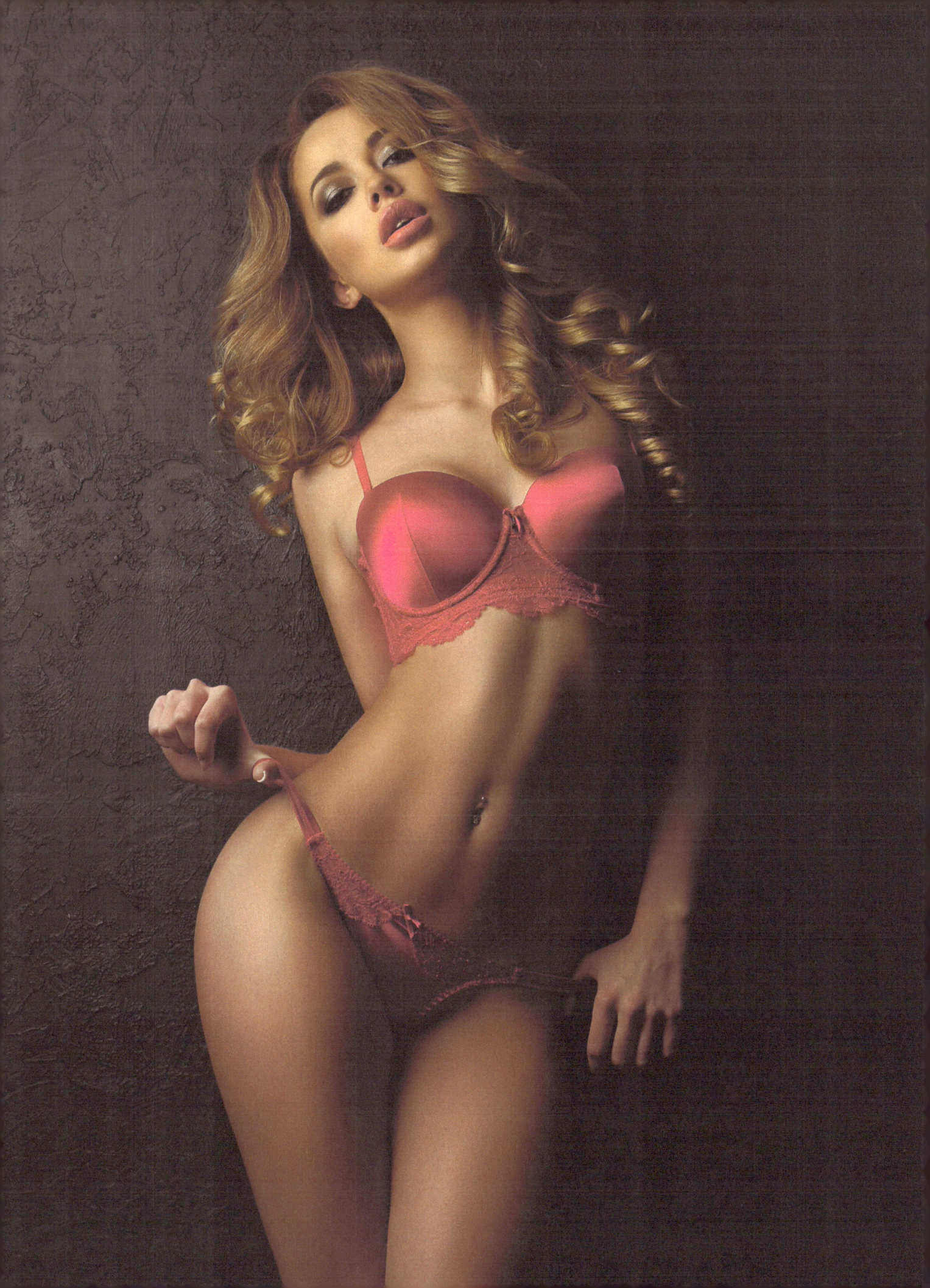

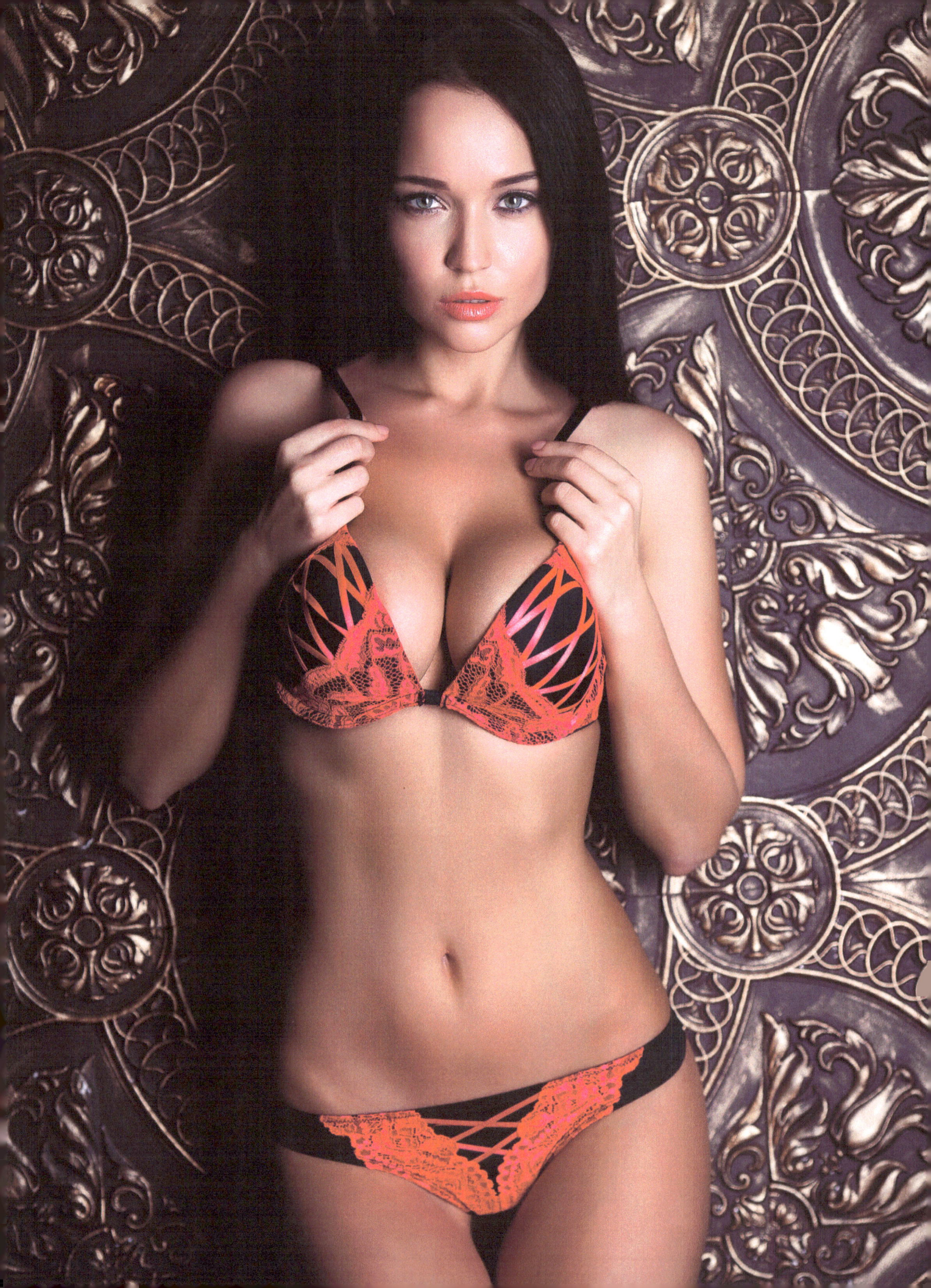

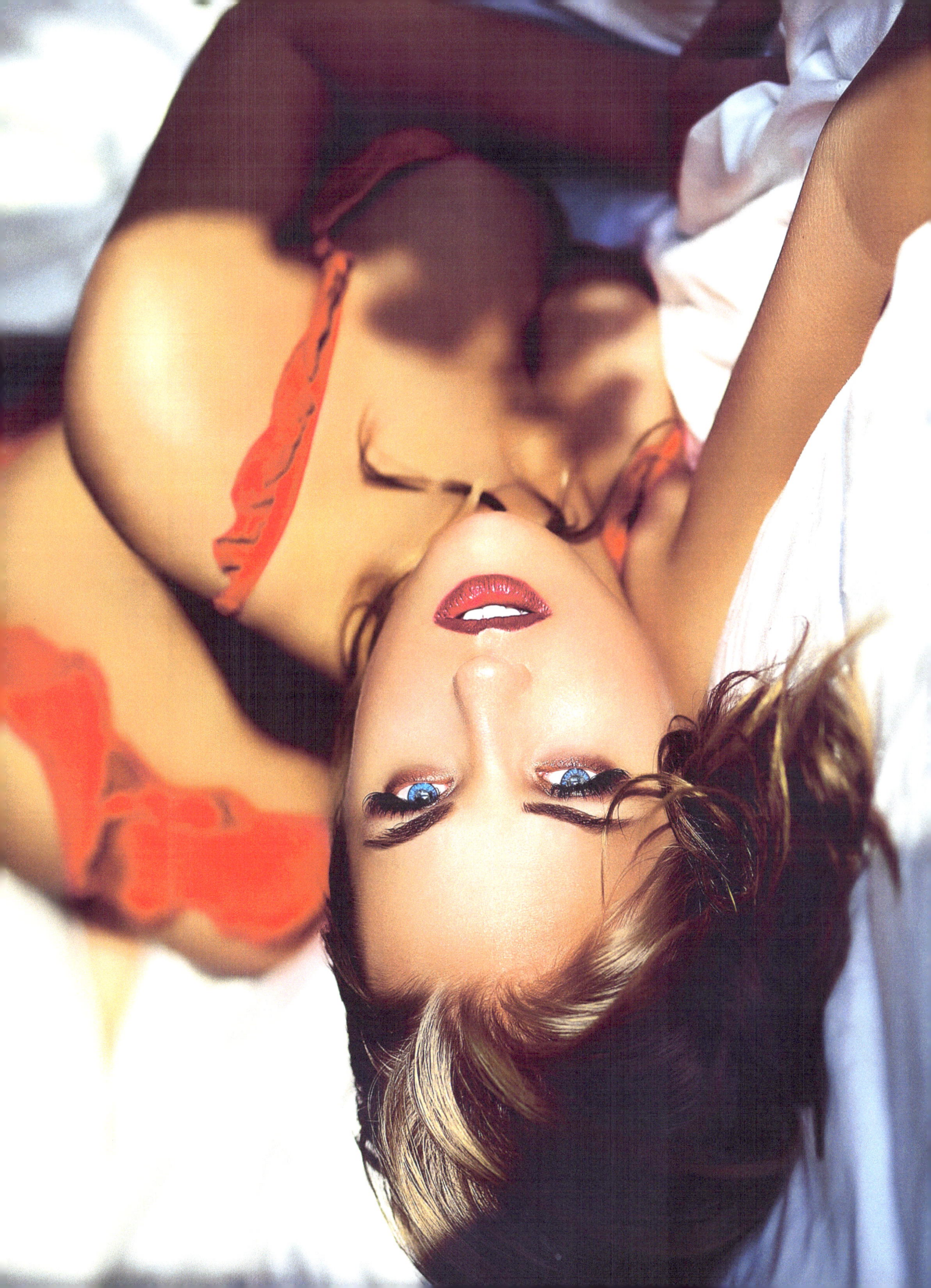

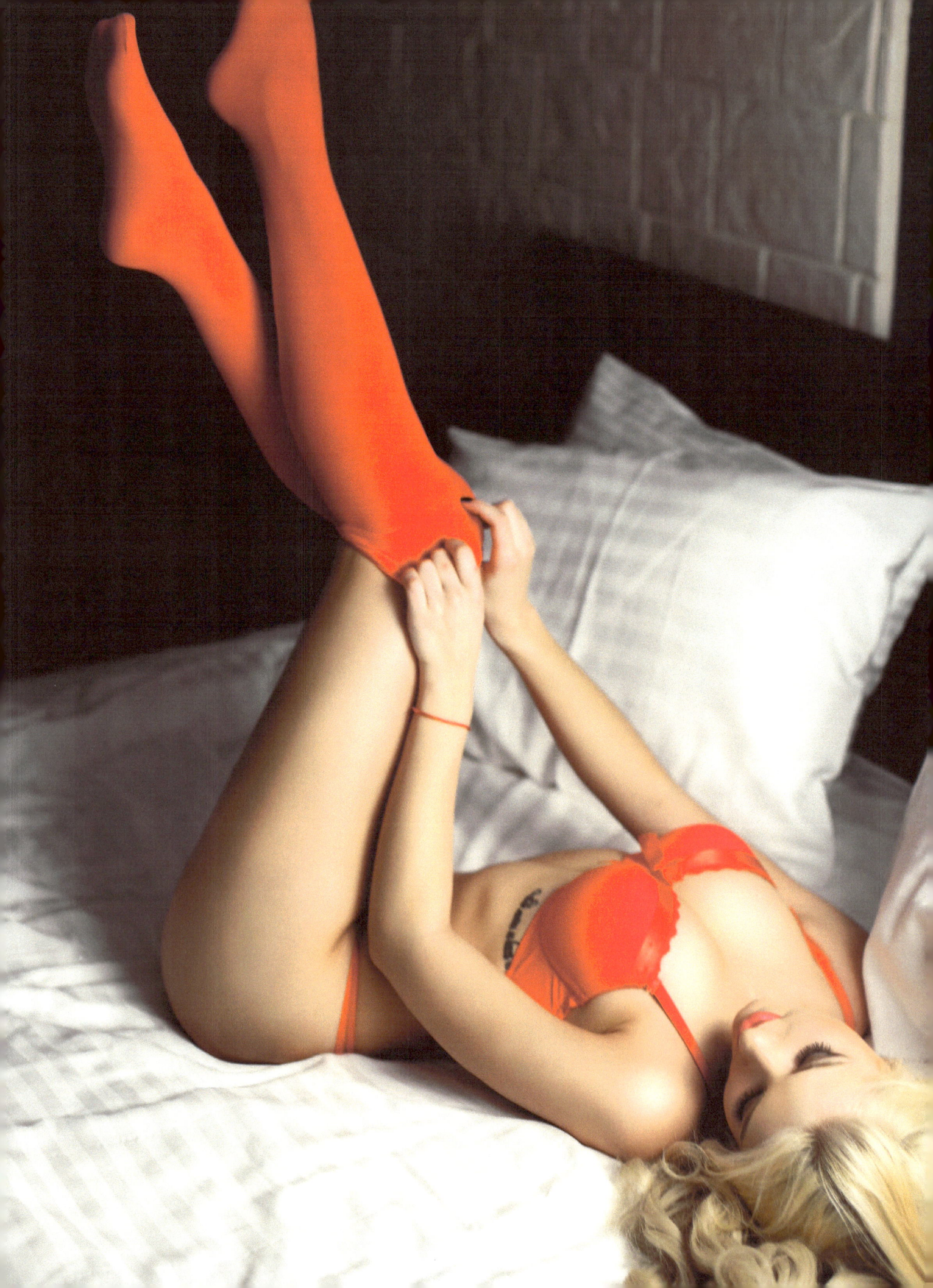

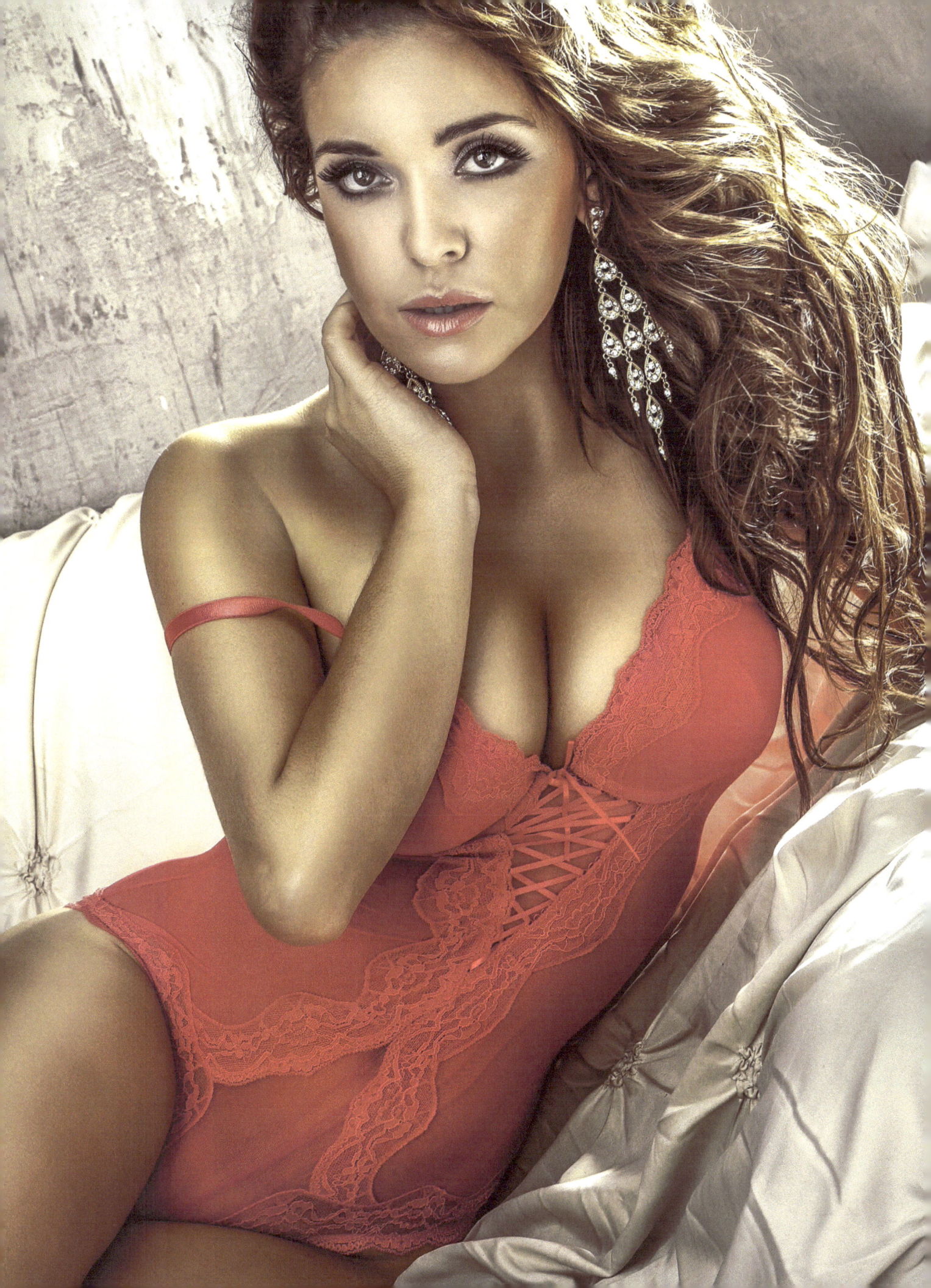

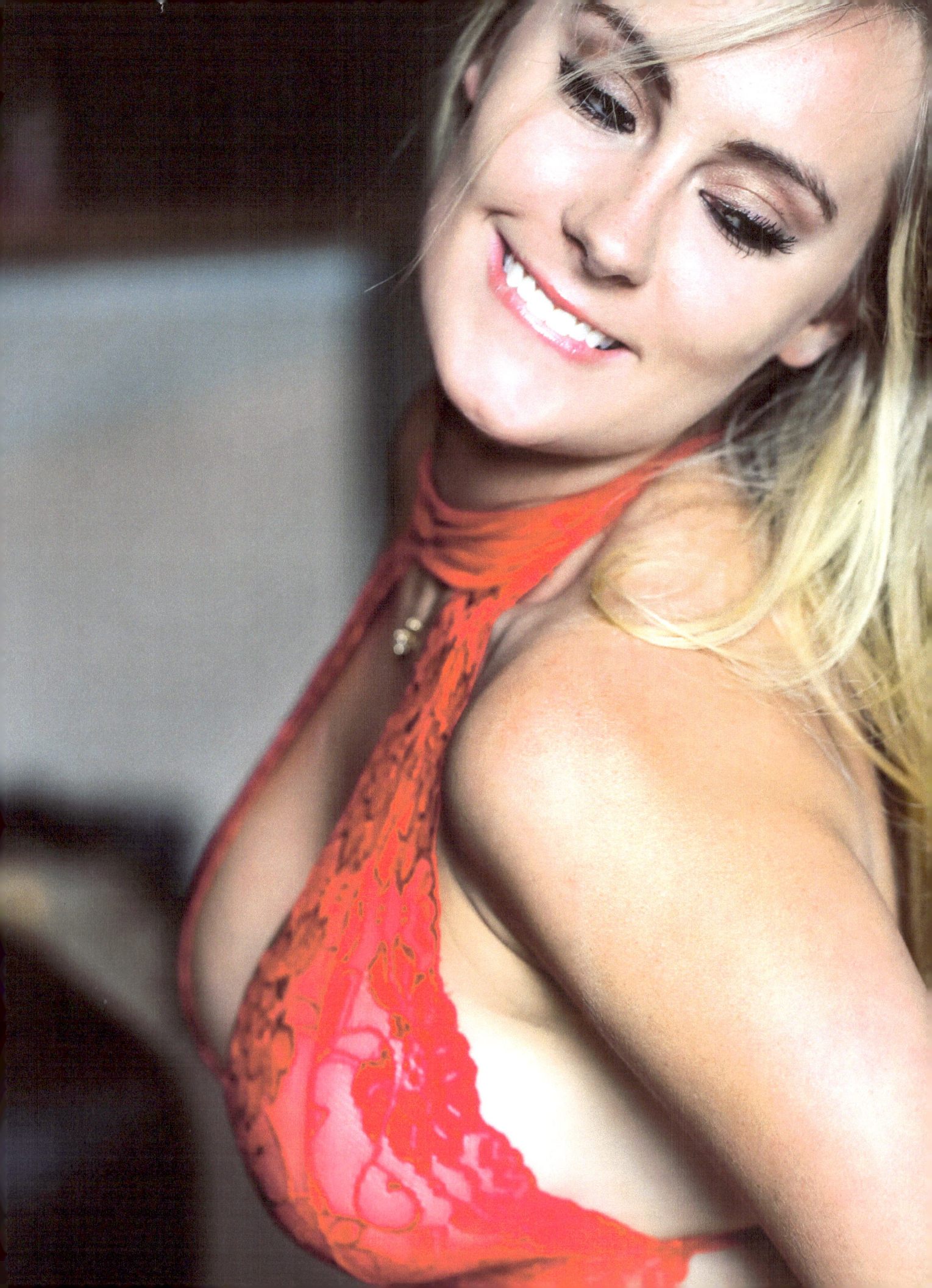

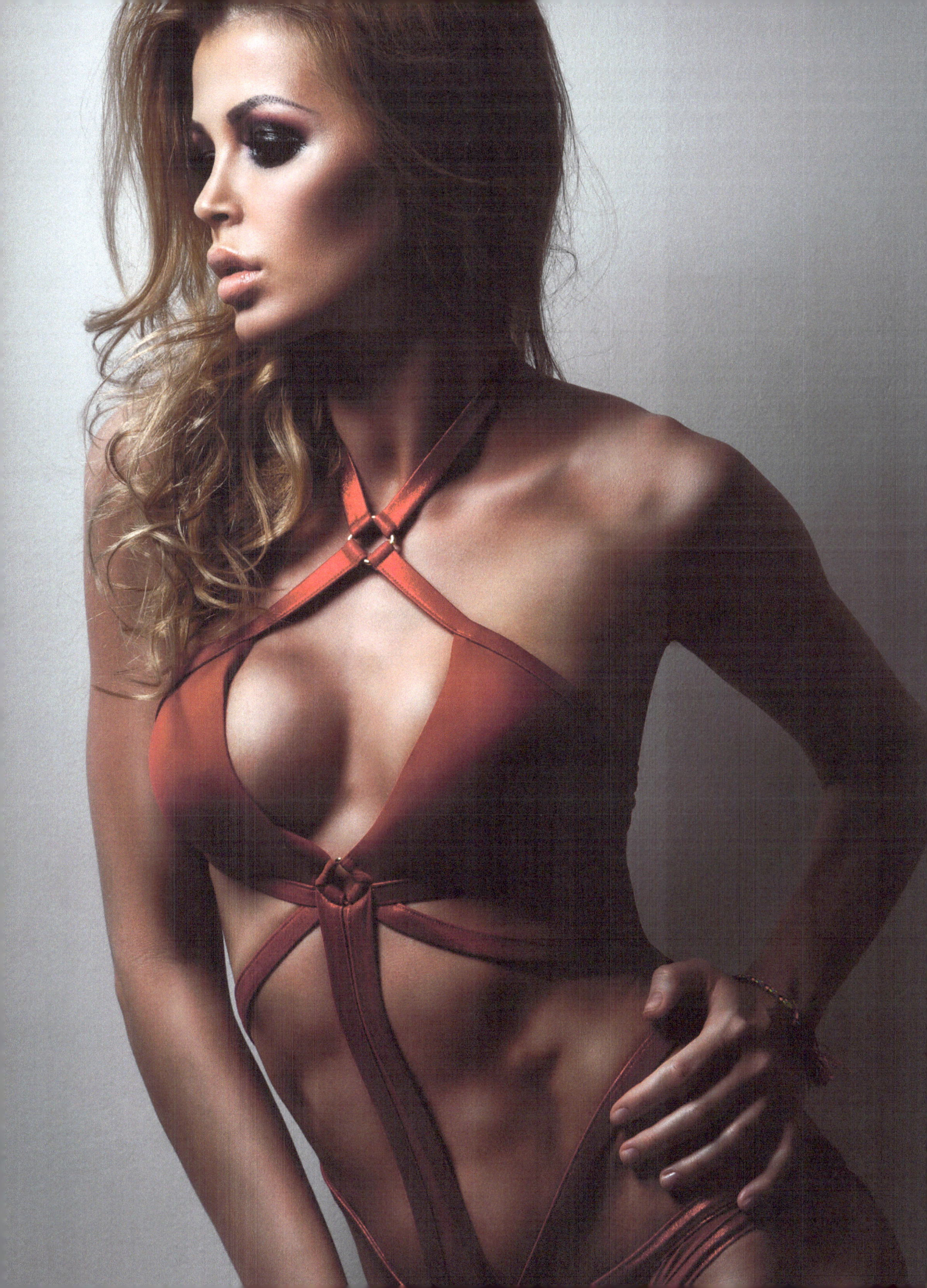

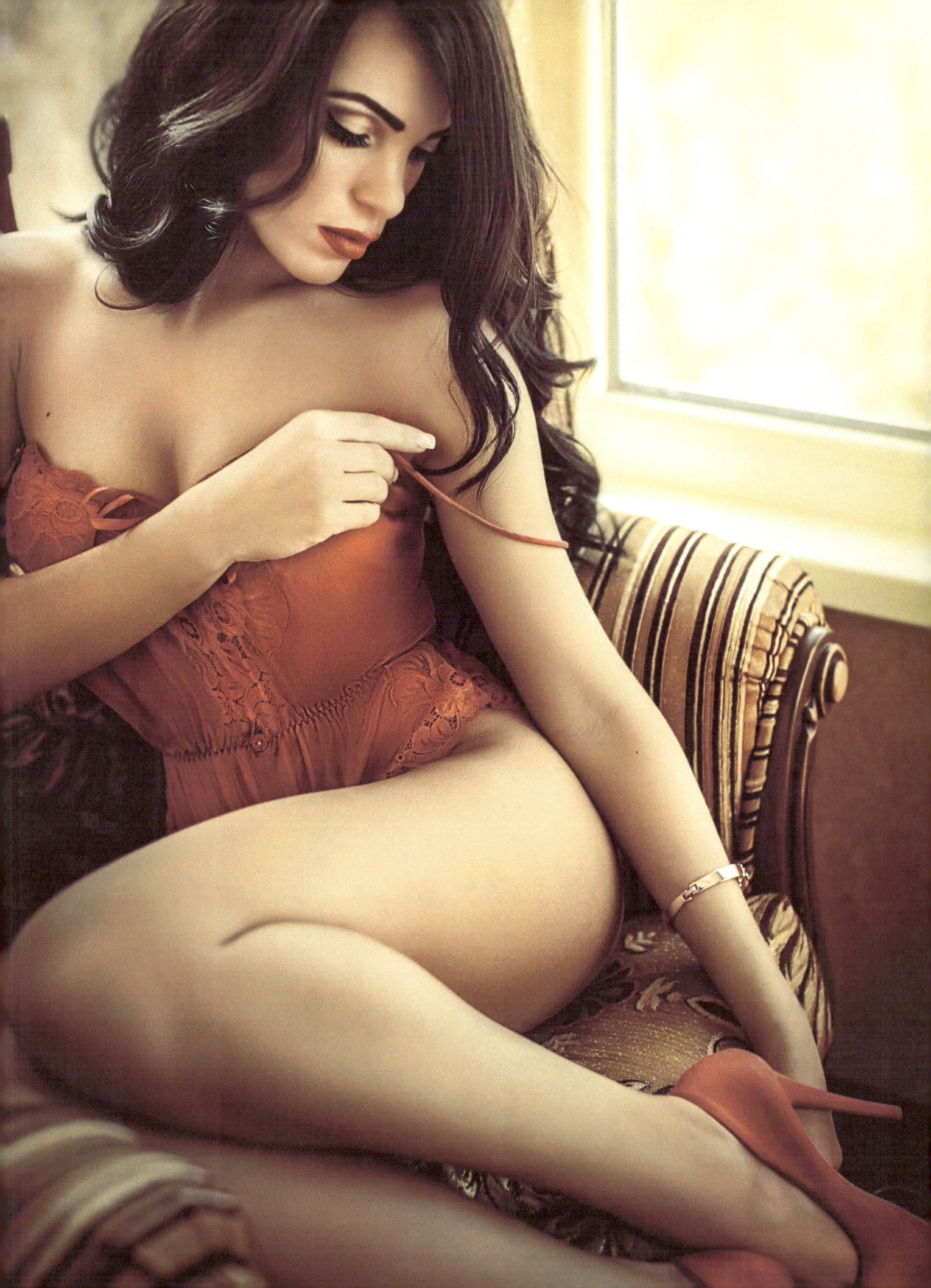

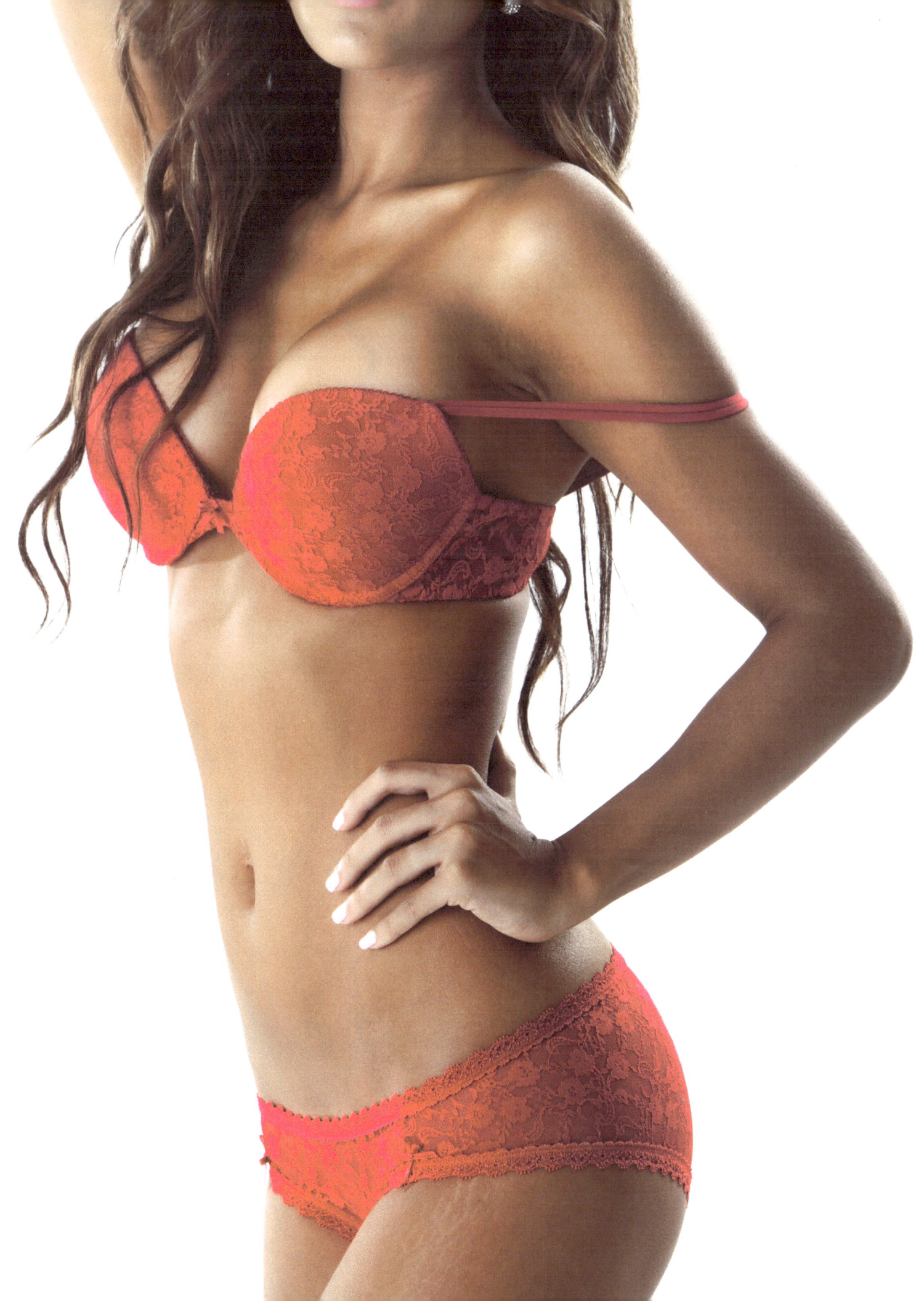

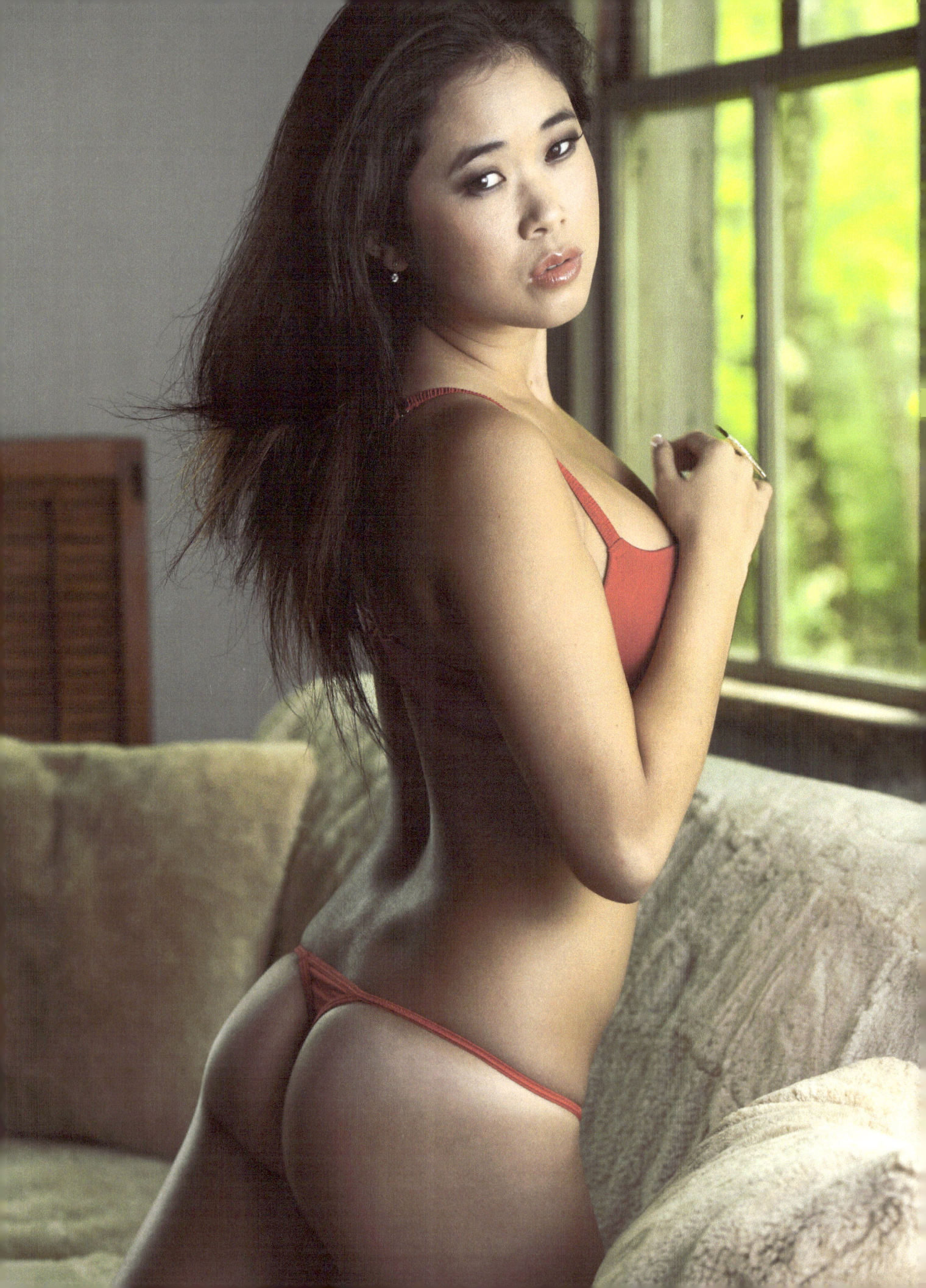

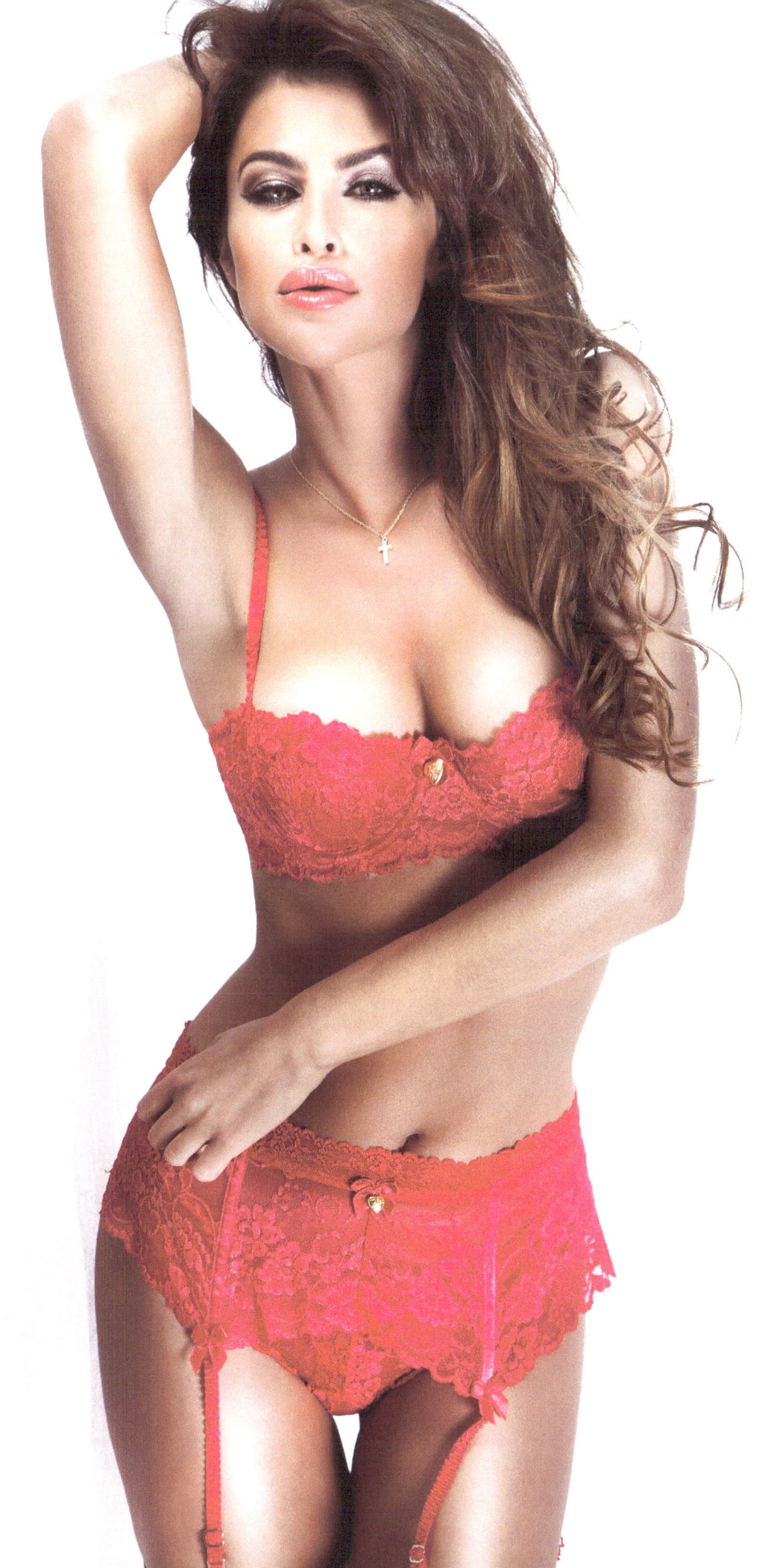

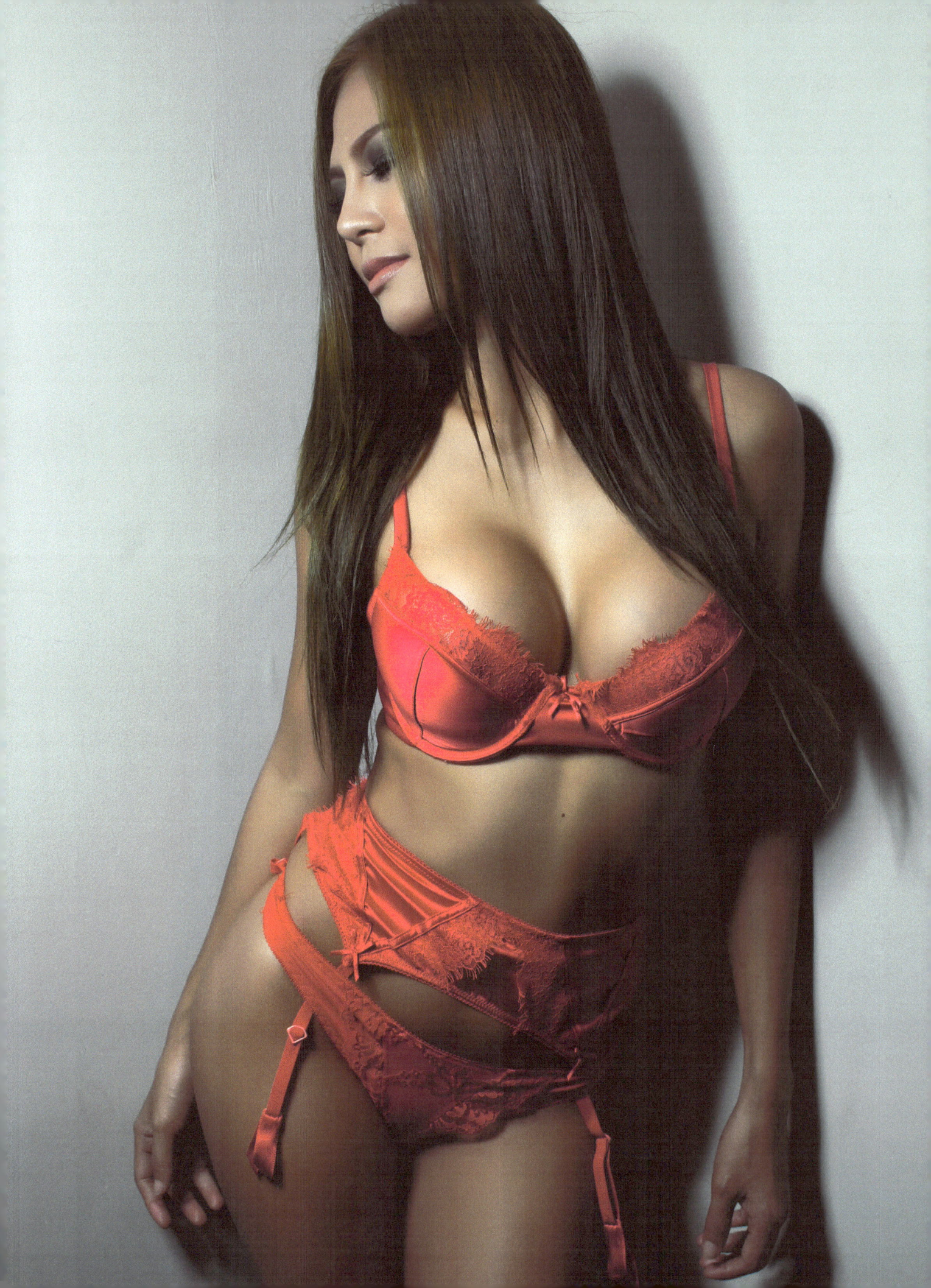

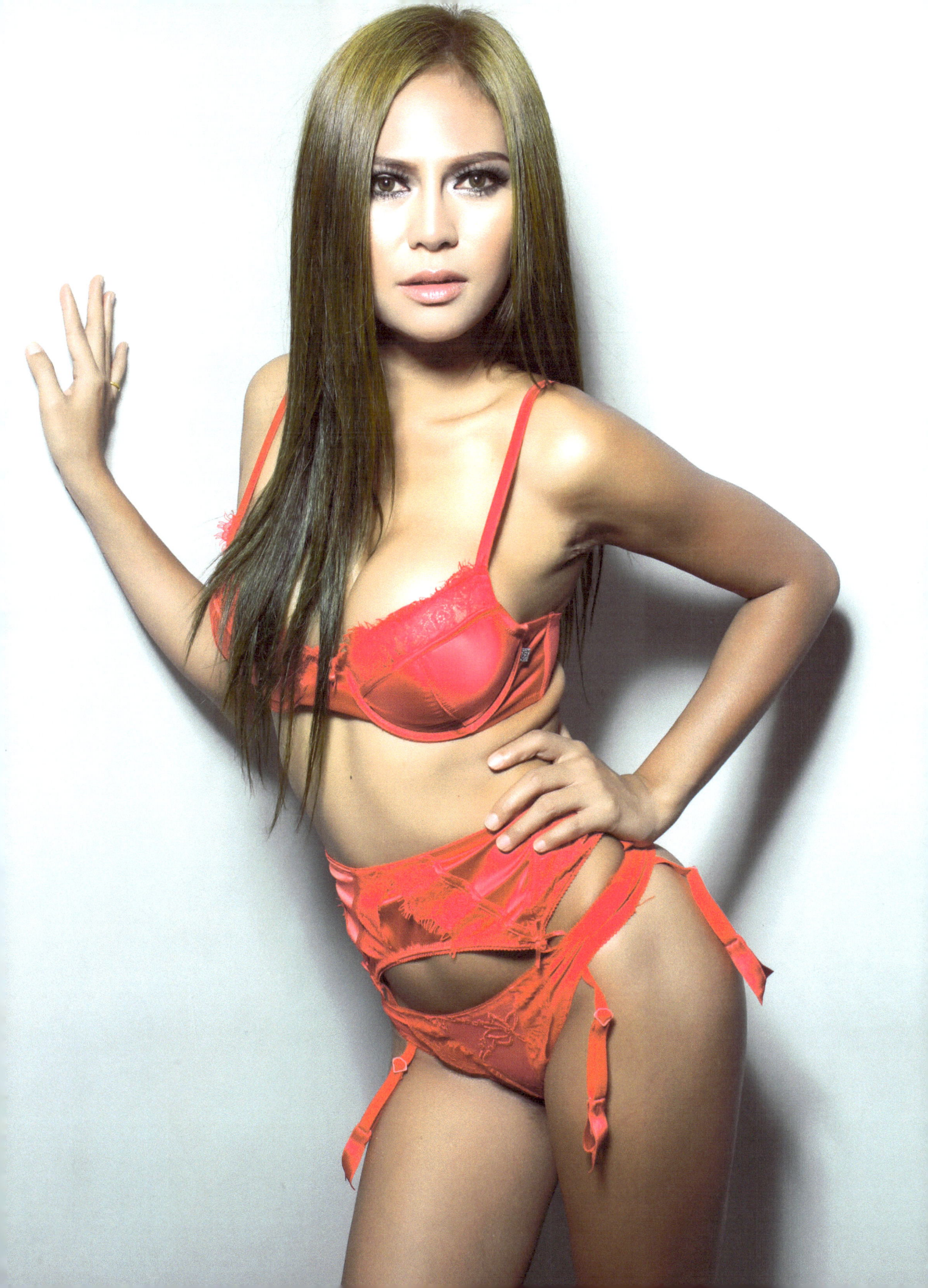

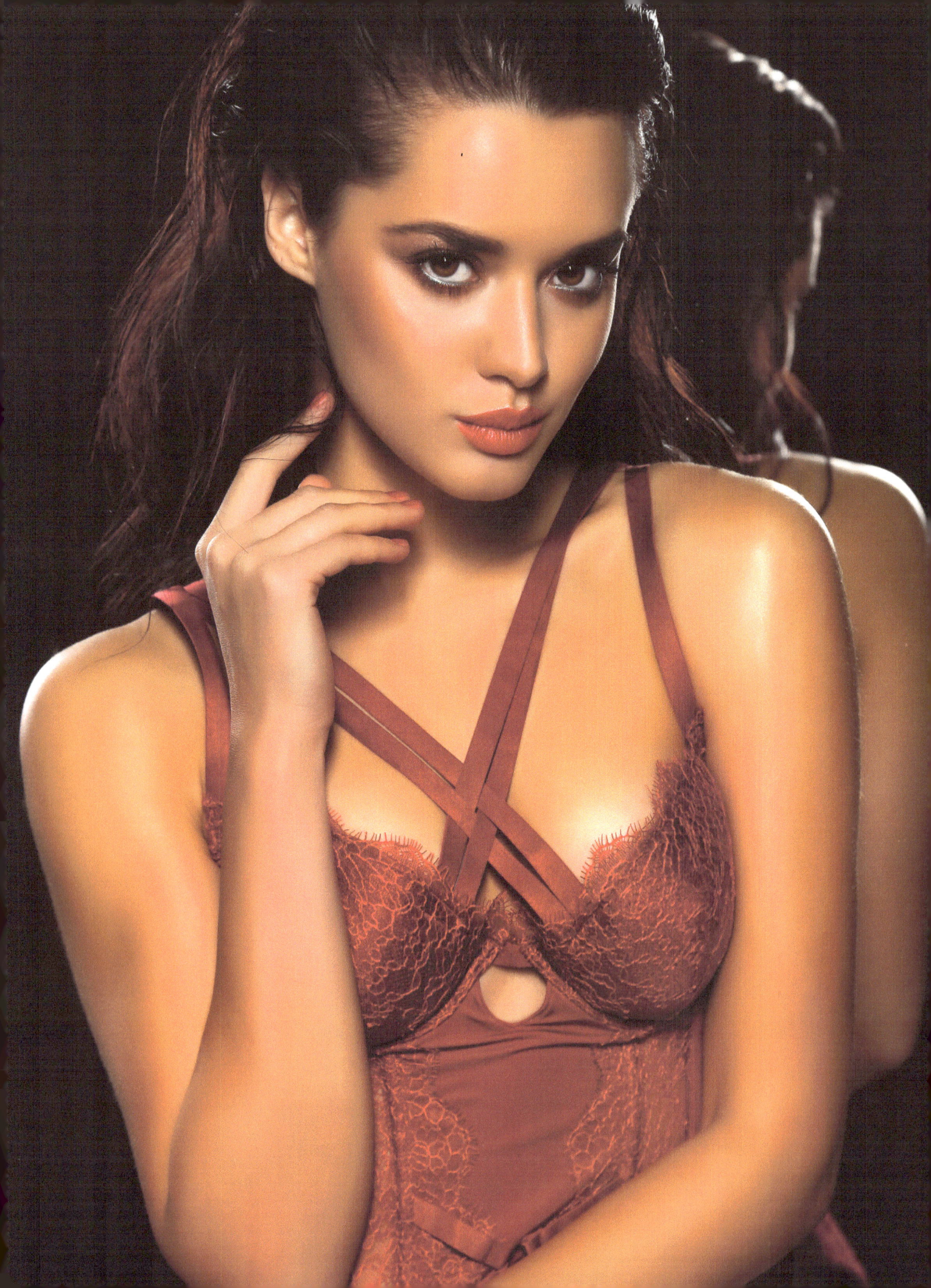

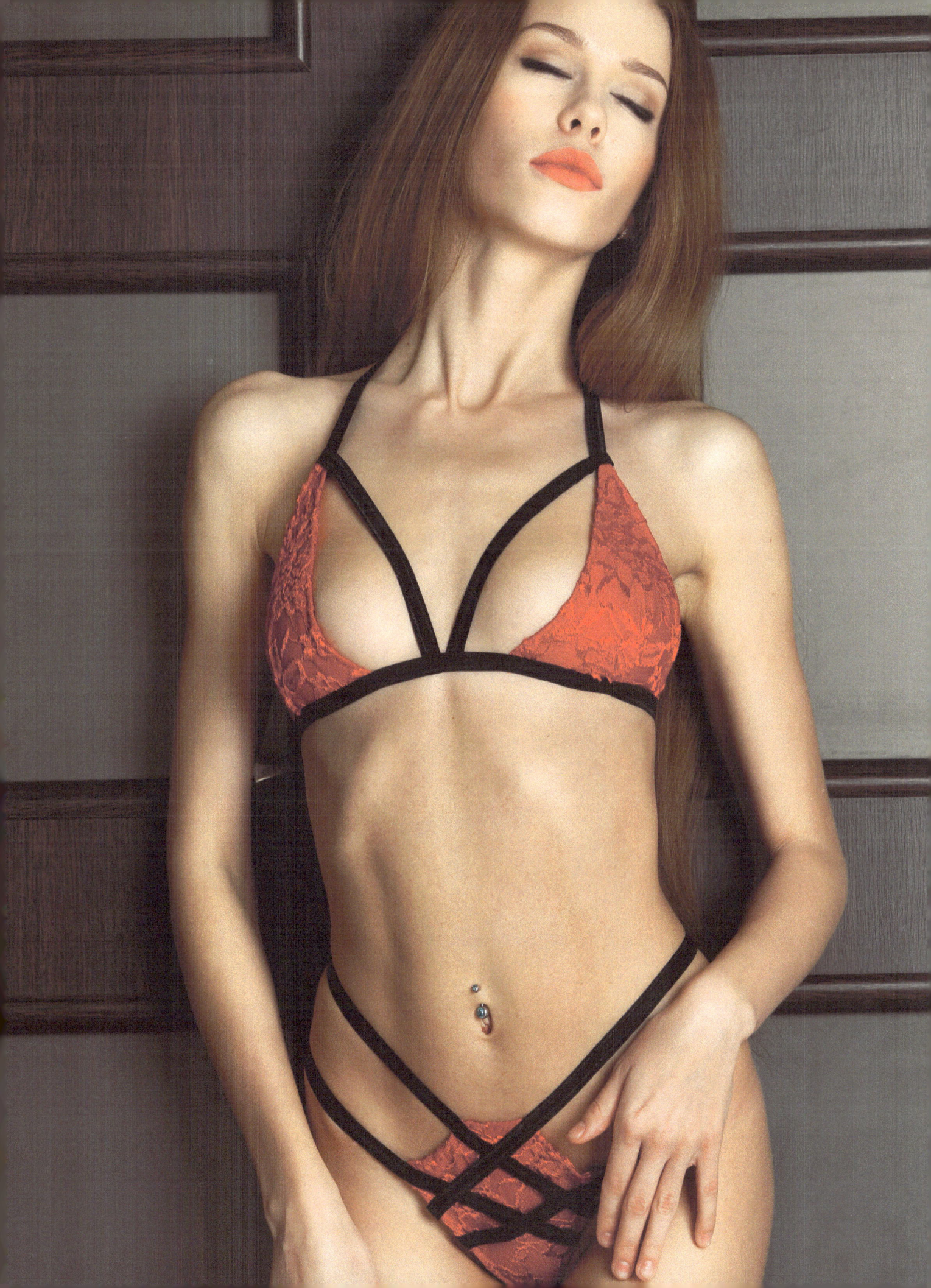

www.ingramcontent.com/pod-product-compliance
Lightning Source LLC
Chambersburg PA
CBHW050421180526
45159CB00005B/2362